Many kids today feel like they don't have a lot of options or tools to positively change or impact the world around them. Maybe you even feel that way, too.

I wrote this book to give you those tools. Because I believe in you and what you want to create. I want you to have what you need to get your voice out *now* because your ideas matter.

And I also happen to believe that creativity can unlock all the good feels in us . . . it's actually the key to living an epic life. Still not convinced? Here's why you should care about tapping into your awesome, creative self:

- All the big innovators who change the world are highly creative people

- Creative people have more fun and live more fulfilling lives

- Thinking outside-the-box opens the door to taking action now instead of sitting around watching things that bum you out

- Doing creative projects kills boredom

- Creative people see possibilities everywhere

Bottom Line: This isn't just any old book that you'll sit and read and think about. This is a book about taking action. I'm going to challenge you to actually DO something. Because you can impact the world from your very own backyard, neighborhood, or school. So express yourself. Get your voice out. I mean, *why wait?* Your thoughts, ideas, and input matter now, like, right this very second.

—from *Art in Action*

MATTHEW "LEVEE" CHAVEZ is the creator of Subway Therapy, an ongoing immersive project at the Union Square subway station in Manhattan. A believer in the therapeutic power of communication and providing people with an opportunity to engage, he has worked in crisis management and education in a variety of different roles, including at a magnet school for students with autism. He is a natural-born listener—strangers have always talked to him on buses, trains, subways, planes, and sidewalks. He is the author of the adult book *Signs of Hope: Messages from Subway Therapy*. He lives in Brooklyn, New York.

www.subwaytherapy.com • @asklevee

BLOOMSBURY PUBLISHING

TITLE: Art in Action: Make a Statement, Change Your World

AUTHOR: Matthew "Levee" Chavez

ISBN: 978-1-68119-756-2

FORMAT: hardcover

TRIM: 5 1/2" x 8 1/4"

HC PRICE: $16.99 U.S./ $22.99 CAN.

PUB DATE: 9/11//2018

TENTATIVE PAGE COUNT: 112

AGES: 10–12

GRADES: 4–6

CONTACT: Lizzy Mason

(212) 419-5340

elizabeth.mason@bloomsbury.com

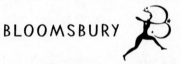

ART in ACTION

Make A Statement, Change Your World

MATTHEW "LEVEE" CHAVEZ

BLOOMSBURY
CHILDREN'S BOOKS
NEW YORK LONDON OXFORD NEW DELHI SYDNEY

BLOOMSBURY CHILDREN'S BOOKS
Bloomsbury Publishing Inc., part of Bloomsbury Publishing Plc
1385 Broadway, New York, NY 10018

BLOOMSBURY, BLOOMSBURY CHILDREN'S BOOKS, and the Diana
logo
are trademarks of Bloomsbury Publishing Plc

First published in the United States of America in September 2018
by Bloomsbury Children's Books

Text copyright © 2018 by Matthew Chavez
Illustrations copyright © 2018 by Allison Steinfeld

Bloomsbury books may be purchased for business or promotional use.
For information on bulk purchases please contact Macmillan Corporate
and Premium Sales Department at specialmarkets@macmillan.com

Library of Congress Cataloging-in-Publication Data
available upon request
ISBN 978-1-68119-756-2 (hardcover) • ISBN 978-1-54760-086-1
(e-book)

Book design by Jeanette Levy
Typeset by Westchester Publishing Services
Printed and bound in the U.S.A. by Berryville Graphics Inc., Berryville,
Virginia
2 4 6 8 10 9 7 5 3 1

All papers used by Bloomsbury Publishing Plc are natural, recyclable
products made from wood grown in well-managed forests. The
manufacturing processes conform to the environmental regulations of
the country of origin.

To find out more about our authors and books visit www.bloomsbury.
com and sign up for our newsletters.

DEDICATION TK

TABLE OF CONTENTS

INTRODUCTION

If you're like a lot of people I know, you skip over the introduction to a book. Because well, you know, it tends to be a little too much blah blah blah and not enough get on with the book already.

So go ahead. Skip it. Challenge normal. And move straight on to the good stuff already. Okay? Cool.

Let's go.

CHAPTER 1

Now THAT WE'VE GOTTEN THAT OUT OF THE WAY . . .

A while ago, I had an idea. This wasn't unusual for me. In fact, I've always been someone with a lot of ideas—for things I want to do, things I want to create, challenges I want to take on, changes I want to make in the world. Sometimes my ideas are, shall we say, way out there, and sometimes they're more practical. Sometimes I let an idea stay in my head, and other times, I just know I've got to bring it to life.

That's what happened the time I decided to bring a small table and two folding chairs with me down into a subway station in New York City. My idea was to create a safe space where people could share something that was weighing them down—a secret, something sad, something worrying them—and walk away feeling a little lighter, freer . . . even happier. And just like that, Subway Therapy was born. Just about every day [I'd head underground and connect with strangers who were curious about what I was up to. Sometimes they'd even sit down to spill out the story of their hopes, their dreams, their problems . . . their life. For the record? I'm not a therapist. But that's okay, because Subway Therapy isn't actually about therapy. It's about creating community where there was none.

When I first got started, I wasn't sure how it was going to go, but something inside told me I had to do it anyway. And I'm glad I did, because over time lots of people started coming by my "office." As my project grew and evolved, I started bringing sticky notes with me for passersby to write or draw on, which gave people a way to turn their big, sometimes stressful, feelings into something beautiful. Each day, these sticky notes—sometimes thousands of them—covered the tile walls of the subway stations, forming huge colorful collages of thoughts, emotions, doodles, and secrets. And when all those notes are stuck up there together, something magical happens. Because they're no longer the words or images of one person. They're a beautiful, collective community art project.

MY "WHY"

You know that awesome feeling you get when someone has really and truly listened to you and cared about what you have to say? I started Subway Therapy because I wanted to be that person for others . . . to give busy, frazzled New Yorkers a meaningful way to engage so they felt less alone and more a part of something bigger. And what do you know . . . it works! Between the people who stop at my table to write out and post a note and the thousands who push the pause button on their harried commute to read a message or two, suddenly strangers from all walks of life are coming together through shared thoughts, feelings, and experiences.

WHAT'S YOUR "WHY"?

Your "why" is your unique motivation for anything you do. To get to know your personal why for an interest of yours, put it through the why test. Just think about something you love to do (a sport, an instrument, a game, a hobby . . . whatever). Got it? Great. Now answer the following questions:

• What excites me most about_____?

• What do I feel when I am doing_____?

• What do I hope will happen because I do_____

Your answers to these questions will shine a spotlight on why you love to do what you love to do, and that knowledge can become the secret to fueling your big ideas.

YOU, YES, YOU, ARE AN ARTIST

So I've got a question for you: Have you ever felt like you had something important to share with the world—a creative idea, an artistic point of view, a special talent or gift—but you didn't know how to do it? If so, a) good, and b) you're in the right place. "Good" because the world is better off when you're sharing your gifts with it, and "you're in the right place" because in this book I'm going to give you my best tips for bringing big ideas to life. The truth is, it's not hard to make something great happen as an artist. In fact, all you need are three simple ingredients—curiosity, creativity, and courage—to make your mark. And my hunch is, you already have them in spades.

I'm here to tell you some BIG NEWS. Are you sitting down? Here it is. Being a creative person or an artist isn't necessarily what you think it is. When I was younger, I thought being an artist meant creating the best projects in art class. Which was a bummer because, honestly, my projects didn't always turn out so well. In fact, if it weren't for the people in my life who supported me in feeling okay about not being the best, I probably would have given up on following my creative passions and I wouldn't be where I am today. Luckily, those people helped me see that art is so much more than a bunch of masterpieces hanging in a gallery.

The truth is, EVERYONE is an artist. (Yes, I'm talking to you.) Because art isn't necessarily something you make—it's what you do in the world. It's dreaming and scheming. It's thinking outside the box and looking at life through your own lens. In a way, being an artist is like being a scientist, because it means you're innovating and trying something new. It means being brave enough to take a chance, even when you don't know how it will turn out or how other people will react.

A NEW DEFINITION OF "ARTIST"

So now that we all agree that you, just as you are, are a creative, artistic person, I'm going to suggest we embrace a new definition of what it means to be an artist. One that has nothing to do with whether or not you can draw well or sing on key or dance en pointe, but instead focuses on

ART IS THE ORIGINAL SOCIAL MEDIA

Subway Therapy is a type of art called social practice, which is a fancy way of saying it takes my creative inspirations and invites other people to be a part of them. Some people call social practice community art, because it depends upon other people to be successful. For instance, when other people participate in what I'm creating, they actually become part of the art. Every person who puts up a sticky note is an artist. And every person who reads even just one note is part of the art too.

Even when I have a day where only one person stops by to read what another person posted, those two people—the writer and the reader—have still made a connection that might never have happened if my project hadn't given them a way to do it. And that matters. Those notes can inspire, comfort, and give hope—pretty amazing stuff, right? Just one voice, your voice, has a big value.

the ways you can share your awesome self with the world. Here's what my new and improved definition includes:

• **Focusing on the process:** I don't want to get all cheesy on you by saying things like "it's about the journey, not the destination," but . . . it's true! Art is about doing, not having done something. The good stuff comes in the process itself.

• **Dropping the expectations:** Artists do their thing without worrying about the outcome. Why? Because at the end of the day (and until mind-influencing technology is developed), we can't control how others will respond to what we're doing. Which leads me to . . .

• **Being curious:** Approaching any creative project with curiosity (i.e., I wonder if people will participate in my project? or I wonder how this idea is going to turn out?) helps artists stay open to the experience instead of feeling stuck or nervous or afraid.

• **Being flexible:** There is no one way art has to look or feel to count as art. And just like a plant grows and changes over time, your art will evolve too. So go with the flow.

WHAT DOES THIS HAVE TO DO WITH YOU, YOU ASK?

I know that many kids today feel like they don't have a lot of options or tools to positively change or influence the world around them. Maybe you feel that way too.

I wrote this book to give you those tools because I believe in you and what you want to create. I want you to have what you need to get your voice out now, because your ideas matter.

And I also happen to believe that creativity can unlock all the good feels in us . . . it's actually the key to living an epic life. Still not convinced? Here's why you should care about tapping into your awesome, creative self:

• All the big innovators who change the world are highly creative people.

• Creative people have more fun and live more fulfilling lives. (It's true!)

• Thinking outside the box opens the door to taking action now instead of sitting around watching things that bum you out.

• Doing creative projects kills boredom.

• Creative people see possibilities everywhere.

Being creative today will pave the way for more success and fulfillment later, since creativity is the single most important ingredient of success. (Need I say more?)

Bottom Line: This isn't just any old book that you'll sit and read and think about. This is a book about taking action. I'm going to challenge you to actually do something. Because you can change the world from your very own backyard, neighborhood, or school. So express yourself. Get your voice out. I mean, why wait? Your thoughts, ideas, and input matter now, like, right this very second.

THE RULES, AKA
"HOW TO USE THIS BOOK"

Like I mentioned earlier, this is no ordinary book. So before you dive in, you've got to read the rules.

- **RULE #1: There are no rules.** That's right. You don't have to read this book in any certain way. You can read it from the front to the back or vice versa. You can do any of the projects you want in any order you want. You can follow the project instructions word-for-word or just use them as a jumping-off point for doing your own in thing in your own way.

- **RULE #2: Think curiosity, not perfection.** In this book I'll share with you what I've learned through trial and error about creating anything you want to create. But you're still going to have to make a few mistakes of your own along the way—that's just how life works. (And often, that's where the really good ideas come from!)

- **RULE #3: Be safe.** Sharing your art with the world requires some extra precautions to make sure what you're doing is positive and safe for you and everyone else involved. (More on that in chapter 7.)

- **RULE #4: Think simple.** You really only need two things to make a statement with your art: you and the person or people you're interacting with. #noexcuses

• **RULE #5: Enjoy the process.** The more you get to creating, the more ideas you'll have, and then the more you'll be inspired to continue moving, shaking, and connecting with others. I bet you fifty bucks that you'll smile during the process.*

Ready? Let's get started!

> **WARNING:**
> The tools provided in this book are powerful. Chances are high that anyone who reads this book will gain the ability to see the world around them as a place of endless opportunities to influence their families and friends, their schools and communities, and maybe even the world. (So what are you waiting for?)

[FN]*This is not a real bet.

CHAPTER 2

UNCOVERING YOUR INNER ARTIST

So how are you feeling?

Ready? Yes.

Inspired? Of course.

Wanna get going? ABSOLUTELY!

Awesome! But first, a riddle: What superpower does everyone have, but not everyone uses?

Anyone? Anyone?

Okay . . . I'll spill the beans. I'm talking about the ability to positively influence the world around us. And unleashing that power begins by uncovering your awesome, creative self. Because truth: you can influence just about anything if you decide that's what you want to do. That's right—you are an agent of change. And you've already got everything you need to do your thing. (It's true.) So let's get to know your inner artist!

THE BIG QUESTION: WHO ARE YOU AS AN ARTIST?

Before you dive in and start spreading your creative goodness everywhere, it's important to get clear on something very important. Namely, who you want to be in the world. (I know . . . big concept, right?) But stick with me.

Since you're going to be out in the world sharing your creativity, the better you understand your vision, your unique perspective, and your personal "why," the bigger an effect your art will have and the more fun it will be creating it.

I know this might seem like a lot to figure out (um, hello . . . existential crisis anyone?), but don't worry—I'm going to break it all down for you. Really, I'm talking about getting clarity around two things: your identity as an artist and your personal brand as an artist. Let's take a look at each one.

YOUR IDENTITY AS AN ARTIST

Let's dial it back for a second. Because "artist" might not even be the word you want to use to describe who you are. In fact, maybe you like one of these better?

- adventurer
- scientist
- explorer
- bohemian
- creator
- entertainer
- community architect
- change maker
- mover and shaker

I just have one favor: No matter what you call yourself, know that you've got the heART of an artist. How do I know? Because you're doing something creative and important to you.

And anyway, the label isn't as important as what you do and how you do it. Letting your creative flag fly means doing things in your own one-of-a-kind way. It means approaching life with the mind-set of a scientist, the curiosity of a detective, and the resilience of an explorer.

When you do this, your identity as an artist can shine through. Here, let me show you what I mean.

- Say a scientist is conducting an experiment, and it crashes and burns. Failure, right? Not so fast—sometimes having things not work can be even more valuable than if they went off without a hitch. In the figuring out what went wrong, it's possible to make an even bigger discovery. The same goes for art.

- Detectives don't already know the answer to the mysteries they're trying to solve. Instead, they're looking at every clue and asking, I wonder what this means? Artists can do the same thing. We don't need to have all the answers before we start—we can approach a project by asking: I wonder what will happen when I create/make/do this?

JOURNAL/DOODLE/DAYDREAM

Get to know your identity as an artist by noodling on these questions:

- What excites me most when I think about being a creative person?

- What kinds of projects am I most curious about creating?

- What message(s) do I hope other people take away from my art?

- What kind of medium(s) feel the most cool and fun to work in?

- Explorers may set off with a plan, but they really don't know which path will get them to their hoped-for destination. (If they did, they wouldn't be explorers . . . they'd be tourists.) Explorers don't give up when they realize they made a wrong turn, and neither should we. We can just try a new direction.

A big part of being curious means tuning in to how you're feeling about what you're doing. If your project starts to feel uninteresting or stressful or like a not-so-fun job, it's probably time to switch gears and try something else. (Makes sense, yes?). Because here's the lowdown—an artist rarely stays the same for long. What makes this so awesome is that it means we get to keep evolving and growing. And that, my friends, is what makes life so interesting!

Oh, one more thing! If you're feeling stuck or unsure about your next big idea—you're not alone. Seriously . . . it happens to the best of us. So if you're trying to come up with the perfect project, I hearby give you permission to take ideas from other artists. I'm talking about using others' creations to inspire your own project. That's right— bust out Google. Look up some of your favorite artists and see what they're up to that you love. I mean, what is it about Bruno Mars's performances that you connect with? What about Banksy's style sparks your creativity? Immersing yourself in the world of creative peeps you admire is sure to get your juices flowing.

When you think about it, there is no such thing as a completely original creative idea—it's next to impossible to not be influenced by other artists. To be sure, you don't cross the line between "being influenced" and "ripping off." Add your own secret sauce and transform an idea so it feels like it's totally you. And if you're not sure where your project lands, put yourself in the other artist's shoes. Would you be upset if someone used your art in the same way?

If you're inspired by another artist and you're thinking of making something super similar, keep it real by:

• sending them a quick note to let them know they inspired you

• contacting them and asking to borrow from their ideas

• giving them credit in your work

YOUR PERSONAL BRAND AS AN ARTIST

Brands aren't just reserved for hip sneakers, pop stars, and soda. In fact, we all have our own special "brand"—a signature style or something that makes us uniquely us. Do you always wear outrageous T-shirts or funky glasses frames? Are you all vegan, all the time? Do your social life and interests revolve around sports? These are all examples of a personal brand. Why does this matter? When your personal brand supports what you're doing in your art, you'll pack a more powerful punch.

Because you are your brand, most everything you do— from choosing your outfit for the day to sharing a photo on Instagram—is a chance to share your brand with the world.

The good news is, you don't have to worry about coming up with an original brand because you already ARE an original.

That's right—the best way to build a brand is by just being yourself. When you do you, you really can't go wrong. The even better news? People respond best to creative projects that feel totally real and authentic. (Makes sense,

POP QUIZ: SO YOU WANT TO ROCK BUILDING YOUR BRAND? ARE YOU . . .

a. the next Selena Gomez?   c. the next Kardashian?

b. the next Subway Therapy?   d. the next Yayoi Kusama?

right? People can spot a faker a mile away.)

None of those feel totally right, do they? Well that's good, because they aren't you. And as it turns out, that's the best advantage you have!

Now that you've let your inner artist out of the bag, it's time for me to share with you my secret creative weapon. That's right—I'm going to show you what's inside my Creative Tool Kit. Ready? Then turn the page.

CHAPTER 3

YOUR CREATIVE TOOL KIT

So what do you need to get started on a creative project? An idea? Well, sure. But it takes more than that to bring your art and creativity into the world. Nope—I'm not talking about paint supplies or an Instagram account or even sticky notes like I used in Subway Therapy. I'm talking about the kind of tools you can't buy or borrow, but are just as important for going from idea to real-world project. I like to call them the Levee Seven.

THE LEVEE SEVEN

Remember how I wrote in the last chapter that creating art isn't so different from being a scientist? Well, as it turns out, the Levee Seven is kinda like my creative spin on the scientific method. Apply these seven steps to your project and you're golden.

Here's what it looks like in action, a la Subway Therapy:

NO. 1: **Observe:** When you use your eyes, are you looking or seeing? (And no, smarty-pants, they're not the same thing.) Looking is noticing the physical stuff—colors, shapes, textures. But seeing? That's going deeper. I'm talking deep-end-of-the-pool deep. As community artists, we want to see how people come across. So instead of tuning in to people's style, hair color, or body shape, we embrace our inner Sherlock and consider expressions and glances and body language the clues. To "see" even further, try thinking about what the world might look like through other people's eyes.

- At first, subway commuters seemed disinterested in one another, but when I observed them more closely, I started seeing clues that they were actually looking for a chance to connect.

NO. 2: Think (and Share) Like Crazy: When you're first forming a new idea, it's like it's floating out there in space with no size or form or color. I love this stage because the idea can unfold in a zillion different ways—it's kind of like a kaleidoscope of possibility, just waiting for you to bring it to life. This is the perfect time to explore your idea with people you trust—your BFF, a sibling, your parents, a favorite teacher—and see what they think. There's something about talking through fuzzy ideas with others that helps them take shape.

- Listening to my close friends' opinions helped me gather the intel I needed to turn my big idea into something real.

NO. 3: Build Your Idea: As you get going with your project, start out simple. At this stage in the game, it's okay if it's not perfect, because nine times outta ten you're going to change it later anyway. Besides, if you worry about having all the bells and whistles right away, you might never get started. Stick to the basics and just begin.

- After I got clear on my idea, I asked myself: What might this look like in the real world? What's the best environment? I settled on something super simple: a table, two chairs, and a sign inviting people to stop and talk.

NO. 4: Try It Out: After you've built it, it's time to be like Nike and just do it. You really can't go wrong no matter what happens—both success and failure give you the info you need to fine-tune your project. Embrace both, and I have no doubt your project will evolve into something wonderful.

• On my first day as a New York Secret Keeper, I tried four different subway stations. By the end of the day, based on what I experienced in each location, I knew which spot was the right one moving forward.

NO. 5: **Listen and Be Open to Change:** As you test out your idea, pay close attention to what the people around you are saying. Other people's feedback might just spark some ideas for how to improve what you're doing. When you keep an open mind and let go of what you think the project should be, you give it a chance to take on an awesome life of its own.

• When I was acting as a Secret Keeper, many people told me that talking with me felt like therapy. I realized they had a point, so I decided to move the project more in that direction and toward what eventually became Subway Therapy.

NO. 6: **Tweak Your Project:** Since you began by laying the groundwork for your project, over time you might want to fill in the details and keep adjusting your idea until it's everything you hoped it would be. Being an artist means you can keep the project growing and evolving, just like you.

• After a while I reworked the details of New York Secret Keeper, changing the name to Subway Therapy and adding my "outfit" of a suit and tie. Even after that, Subway Therapy has continued to change in little ways, which makes the project more fun, both for me and the public.

NO. 7: **Go Back to the Beginning:** I'm not saying you need to scrap your idea and start from scratch. (Though that's always a possibility!) But I am saying it's worth rewinding every now and then to think about how things are going, decide whether you want to make any changes, or dig into a new idea. Whichever way you go, go knowing you can always start over. That doesn't mean you've failed—it means you're giving yourself the gift of a fresh start.

CHAPTER 4

PROJECTS AT HOME

Family—you know, the people you pass the salt to at dinner, go on vacations with, share the bathroom with—is the very first community you're a part of. No matter what your family looks like—traditional or alternative, close knit or distant, blood relatives or other caregivers—the people you share a life with shape who you are and how you see the world from the get-go.

And like any community, family life comes with different rituals, expectations, and routines. Friday pizza nights, Sunday breakfast bagels, a bath and reading after dinner;

Saturday chore days, after-school dog walks, game nights. While routines like these can keep things humming along smoothly, sometimes they get in the way of spontaneity and creativity.

So let's shake things up then, shall we?

Before you get too excited, I'm not talking about boycotting chores or switching out pizza for pasta. I'm talking about inviting your family to be a part of your creative projects. No doubt they're already clued in to your steady supply of artistic energy, but they may not realize they can be a part of it too. And when you inject your creativity into your home, the results can be off the hook.

So, voilà! Here are a few reasons why bringing your art into action at home can have a big effect t (even beyond the walls of your house or apartment):

A. Home is usually a safe place to try out your own brand of community-style art. I'm sure your fam already thinks you're pretty awesome, but seeing you in your groove is the kind of thing that gives parents and caregivers all the f good feels. Not to mention there's a high chance someone in your family bought this book for you in the first place. So why not give some of that love right back?

B. Sharing your art with your family will make your home life feel more comfy, creative, and connected. Together, you'll have new things to talk about and fresh ways of going about the usual day-to-day stuff. (P.S. This is the secret sauce to never having a boring day.)

C. You'll not only learn more about why you are the way you are, but you'll get to know your parents or caregivers on a whole new level too. After all, the adults in your life are more than just your chauffeur or washer of dirty clothes or signer of permission slips. My guess is they have more layers than an unpeeled onion! Plainly put, your family is made up of creative people too. And unleashing their creative side can only be a good thing, yes?

Freeze! I know what you're thinking. (Yes, I'm that good.) You're thinking: Wait a second, I thought we were going to use our art to make the world better. This sounds like I'm still in my own home. Well here's the deal. It may look like we're starting small, but bringing art into your family has the potential to do so much more. Because when the people around us feel more creative, it influences everything in their lives too. And just like a good joke or a bad rumor, creative energy can spread. But even more than that, all these reasons equal your gaining more confidence, which means you'll be all set for having a BIG influence in the outside world. And that, my friends, is what we're going for.

PROJECT: THE FAMILY INTERVIEW

For when you want to feel like an investigative journalist, historian, or scholar

WHAT: Become an investigative journalist by interviewing family members or other people in your life about a topic you're especially curious about—your family history, current events or politics, or even just life in general—and turn it into art you can share.

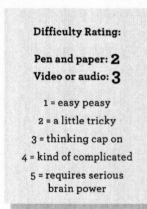

Difficulty Rating:

Pen and paper: 2
Video or audio: 3

1 = easy peasy
2 = a little tricky
3 = thinking cap on
4 = kind of complicated
5 = requires serious
   brain power

WHERE: Anywhere your interview subjects are (home, school, neighborhood, relatives' house, etc.), or over Skype or FaceTime.

WHY: Being an investigative journalist is a great way to get answers to your burning questions, get to know someone on a deeper level, better understand a topic you're curious about, or show the world how secretly awesome another person is. You might even discover a fascinating secret along the way (people often end up spilling the beans once they get talking!).

WHAT YOU NEED

Pen and paper version
- pen or pencil
- notepad, journal, or anything else to write on

Video version
- cell phone camera or other video recorder
- computer or tablet
- editing software

Audio version
- cell phone recording app or other audio recorder
- computer or tablet
- editing software

WHO YOU NEED

Whoever you want to interview!

HOW TO DO IT

1. Choose a topic: What kinds of things are you most curious about? What subjects do you want to learn more about? Choose a topic or two to explore in your interview.

2. Find an interview subject: Who do you want to interview? Once you know whose brain you want to pick, ask them if they're game and set up a time for the interview.

3. Pick a medium: How do you want to share what you uncover with the world? For instance, if you're curious about how to bake, you might interview someone about their favorite recipes and create a simple recipe book. If you want to know more about your family history, you might record the interview using audio or video and turn your content into a documentary or podcast.

4. Write up your questions: What do you want to know? Come prepped with a list of questions so you don't forget anything important during the interview.

5. Conduct the interview: Step into journalist mode and ask away, recording the responses on paper, a computer, or another recording device.

6. Transform and share your conversation: After you're finished with the interview, it's time to turn the info you

BONUS TIP:

If the people around you aren't up for answering the questions you're most curious about, don't stop there—find someone who is, like a specialist or expert. Because (little known secret) people love talking about their passions.

For tips on how to reach out cold to strangers and up your chances of getting a response, check out page X in chapter 7.

gathered into art. Get creative: make a book, a newspaper, or a zine; create a documentary or a podcast or slideshow. Find ways to add interesting touches to the project with things like pictures, music, and the little details that make the project more you. Then host a screening, blast your podcast out on social media, or present your creation to people in (and maybe outside of) your world.

INTERVIEWING 101—TOP TIPS

Go pro by following these tips for a great interview:

- Find a time that works for both you and your interview subject. Best times are when neither of you will be stressed, rushed, or distracted.

- Choose the interview spot thoughtfully (i.e., somewhere not too loud and where you'll both feel comfortable answering personal questions).

- Avoid "yes" or "no" questions that will result in a bunch of one-word answers. Instead, try phrases like "Can you describe . . . ?" and "Tell me about . . . " or "What are your ideas about . . . ?"

- Don't be afraid to go off-script. If your interview subject says something unexpected and interesting, go with the flow and see where the conversation takes you.

PROJECT: FAMILY TREE

For when you want to make your family roots come alive

WHAT: Challenge what you know about traditional family trees and make something truly unusual using materials that are special and individual to your family.

WHERE: In your home. (You know, your pad . . . your crib . . . that place where you live.)

WHY: When we think about our family roots, we tend to think about a long line of great-great-great-great-great-great-great-great-(you get the picture)-grandparents. But what if there was another way to explore who you are and where you come from, and tap into your family pride? This Family Tree project shines a spotlight on the connection you have with your home and family right now, like this very second.

WHO YOU NEED
• your family or people you live with

WHAT YOU NEED
• materials that represent you and your family (I'll talk more about what this can look like in a second . . . keep reading!)

HOW TO DO IT

1. Pick your brain: Before you even get started, take time to toss some ideas around inside your head to figure out a direction for the project. Since there are approximately a billion ways to create this kind of family tree, thinking about the following questions, which can help you home in on what feels like a cool approach for you:

- What do I love most about my family or where I live?
  - Can you think of some creative ways to represent those things?
  - Are there objects around your home that represent those things?
- What do I want someone else to see, think, or feel when they look at my family tree?
  - Will they understand more about you and your family?
  - Do you want them to feel like they totally "get you"?

MAKE IT A FAMILY AFFAIR

Don't forget to ask people in your family to be a part of creating this project too. What items would they include? What would they most want someone else to know about your family? What do they see as the things that set your family apart from the rest? Remember—this is a family tree, not just a one-totally-awesome-amazing-kid tree. The other peeps in your family are literally a part of the art, so why not give them a voice in how it turns out?

2. **Collection time:** Start gathering content for your creation. Again—think no rules. Your family tree might be made up of actual physical objects—travel mementos, old birthday cards, dice from a favorite family game, photographs. Maybe you want to go poetic and pepper it with quotes, silly sayings, or jokes that are often heard inside your home. Your family tree might include music, recorded voices, or video clips that totally express your family's one-of-a-kind vibe. One you've gather your materials, step back and take a look at what you've got. Is there a logical way these pieces are coming together already?

3. Build away: It's time to create your Family Tree! Remember: Your tree can look however you want it to look. Big, small; flat art, three-dimensional; interactive or old school. Free your inner artist and see where the process takes you. In my experience, any path you go down is a good one.

> **BONUS TIP:** Don't stop now! If you loved this project, great! And know that it doesn't have to end here. You can take this same idea of a family tree, but instead of focusing on your little family unit, amp it up and create a community tree that tells the story about the place you live. I'll even give you a boost—try asking people in your neighborhood what they love most about it. See if that leads your imagination anywhere!

PROJECT: THE PATCHWORK STORY
For when you want to feel like a storyteller

WHAT: Craft an imaginative story written one line at a time with the help of your family or other people in your home. Each person takes turns adding lines to the story, building on what the previous writers created.

Difficulty Rating: 5

1 = easy peasy

2 = a little tricky

3 = thinking cap on

4 = kind of complicated

5 = requires serious brain power

WHERE: On a piece of paper posted on the refrigerator or laid out on the dining room table, or on a chalkboard wall or whiteboard in your house.

WHY: While it's fun to express your creative side in the way only you can, teaming up with others in your family every now and then is a great way to connect, get silly or deep, and even see each other in a whole new way. Who knows . . . you just might discover a side to someone you never even knew existed!

WHAT YOU NEED
- something to write the story on
(paper, chalkboard, whiteboard)
- a way to post the story, such as magnets, tape, tacks, or string
- pencils, pens, chalk, or markers

HOW TO DO IT
1. Get ready: Decide where you want your story to live and how you want the creative flow to go. For instance, will you use different-colored markers for each line a different person writes?

2. Invite your participants: You'll need to clue your family or housemates into the idea of the patchwork story and walk them through the guidelines:
- One at a time: Each person can only write one line at a time.

- No double turns: You can only write after someone else has written another line.
- No time limits: Come and go as you please—you can write whenever you feel like it.
- The end: There is no minimum or maximum length for the story. When it feels finished, it usually is!

3. Set up your station: The easier you make it to participate, the more likely people will! So pick a spot where the story can't be missed and set up your writing station.

4. Start with a bang: Write an interesting, but easy-to-follow, first line of the story. Remember, sometimes people forget how to be creative—it's up to you to give them a boost (see the following page to give you some ideas to get you started)!

Participate! Since this project is for everyone, you should enjoy it too. Think of yourself as the publisher of the story—you can definitely be one of the writers, but your main job is to keep things interesting and move the story along. (I've got tips for you on how to do just that coming up!)

If your patchwork story is falling flat, be a rogue writer and influence the story by keeping the flow on track. Your co-authors will never have to know, but my hunch is they'll soon notice they're more engaged than they were before. Go you!

ONCE UPON A TIME IS SO OVERDONE

Kick off your story with something outside the box. Here are some ideas to borrow or remix and make your own:

• The family was walking down the street just minding their own business when they saw ...

• It started out like any other trip to the grocery store until ...

• The big golden dog was happily napping in the sun when ...

• Mikey and Mary were having the best time at the park with their ...

• B-man the alien was working on his math homework when ...

5. The End. You've finished the story. So now what? You get to choose what you wanna do next. Do you want to ...

• Keep it? You can save the written story and hang it up somewhere for all to see, or maybe you want to take a picture of it or type it up on the computer. If you're feeling super ambitious, you can even turn it into a real book (work with your folks to find some online companies to print it out).

• Redo it? So you loved it, right? Well then, by all means, start from scratch and do it again!

• Bag it? Didn't go so well? That's okay too. You can try again with your family, move onto something else, or give it a whirl with a group of friends to see if you have more success.

MAKING A GREAT STORY

If the story goes off the rails or you can tell your co-authors are getting bored, inject a dash of tension or drama, like having your character come up against a big obstacle. In fact, a stellar story always has these elements:

- **Introduction:** The part that sets up the story with details about things like characters and setting.

- **Rising Action:** The part that develops the problem or conflict through events that build interest or suspense.

- **Climax:** The part where the conflict reaches its peak and changes everything (otherwise known as the "turning point").

- **Falling Action:** The part after the climax that inches the story closer to the resolution.

- **Resolution:** The part where the problem or conflict is solved (and they all live happily ever after . . . or not!).

PROJECT: HIDDEN MESSAGES

For when you want to connect with the people around you

WHAT: Write a message for someone in your family, then hide it in your home for them to discover. Invite them to respond back with their own hidden notes.

Difficulty Rating: 3

1 = easy peasy
2 = a little tricky
3 = thinking cap on
4 = kind of complicated
5 = requires serious brain power

WHERE: Anywhere in your home, on anything you can write on.

When you talk to someone every day, it's easy to fall into a routine of how to communicate and what you talk to each other about. This is a way to shake it up! Communicating with your family in a new way might inspire you to have conversations you never would think to have in person.

WHAT YOU NEED
- paper
- pencils, pens, or markers

HOW TO DO IT
1. Think about it: Who do you want to write to and why? Do you want to ask a question that you are too shy to ask in person? Do you want to tell someone how much they mean to you? Or do you want to share a story and brighten someone's day?

2. Write it: Put your thoughts to paper. At the end of your message, make sure that you ask the recipient to write back to you. You could even include an extra piece of paper and a pen to make it super easy to respond. The invitation part is very important; this is what opens the door for a conversation.

3. Hide it: When you're just starting out, leave notes in places where they are easily found. You might want to include the person's name on the front, or you can fold it up and write "open me" to be extra sure your recipient will know to pick it up.

4. Wait!: If more than a week has gone by and you haven't gotten a response of some kind, ask the person if they found your note. If they didn't, let them know a message is waiting for them and give them a hint on how to find it. If they did, ask them if they want to write something back. Maybe they already have and you haven't found it. Or maybe they just don't know what to say yet. You can try again—this time you might ask a specific question for them to respond to. Doing new creative things can be challenging for people, so the easier you can make it for them to participate, the more likely it is that they will continue to participate.

MIX IT UP!

Once you and your partner have gotten better at hiding notes, switch it up! Think about changing from hiding your notes on a piece of paper to leaving them on other objects in the house—write a message on the lid of an egg carton or on the bottom of a tissue box. Of course, be sure not to write on anything permanent without asking permission.

BONUS TIP:

You could just fold your paper up into a square, but why not get a little fancy and use an origami pattern? Here's an origami dog to try.

1. Place your paper on a flat surface with corners pointing at the top and bottom. Fold it in half from side to side to form a triangle, then unfold it. You should be able to see a crease.

2. Now fold it in half from the top to bottom to form another triangle. Leave this one folded.

3. Fold the tips of the top two corners down—these are your dog's ears. You can fold them down far to make floppy ears or just a little bit for short perky ones.

4. Lift the top layer of paper at the bottom and fold the tip of the point up. Then fold once more to tuck in the tip. Now you have a nose.

5. You've got an origami dog! You can decorate the dog by drawing on eyes, ears, or anything else you would like. Don't forget to include your message! Turn the dog over and write it on the back.

CHAPTER
5

PROJECTS AT SCHOOL

Sometimes so much of school life can be about what's happening on the outside—how you dress, what kind of phone you use, what sports teams you're on, which role you landed in the class play, whether you're friends with the cool kids or the nerds or the artsy-fartsy types. But all this stuff? It's all surface level (or what I sometimes refer to as . . . boring).

You and I both know there is so much more going on with you and the other kids at school. You know that while, yes, school can be rough for a number of reasons, it can also be awesome because these are the years when you and your friends are figuring out who you are and how you plan to shake up the world. You know that being your bold, awesome self is where it's at, and that real is the new cool. So why not lead the way?

Love it or hate it, school is a big part of your life. And by big, I mean BIG. We're talking, if you're like most kids, you spend around a thousand hours each year there. But regardless of whether you're kicking butt in your studies, you're more into the social scene, or you're biding your time until you can move on to the next grade and whatever comes next, you can amp up your experience and make school way more interesting by seeing it for what it is—a perfect venue for engaging in some seriously cool community art. The kind of art that can make a scene, in the best possible way.

Here are just a few reasons why bringing your creativity to your class absolutely rocks:

A. You can have a lot of influence. Not only can you add some pep into the same old class–lunch–more-class routine, but as you'll see from the projects that follow, you might actually help change the culture of your school in a positive way by making it a more friendly or accepting place. That's right—actual world-changing goodness can start inside the double doors of your school. (And how cool is that?)

B. You have a (mostly) captive audience. Of course not

everyone at your school has to join in with what you're doing, but you'll still have a large pool of diverse kids who might be interested in participating.

C. You might get bonus credit for a class. No promises, but who knows? Depending on the project you do and the classes you have, it may be possible to earn some brownie points (and is that ever a bad thing?).

Read on for my favorite community art projects that are perfect for spicing up school life in fun, fresh, and creative ways. Changing the school culture can start with you!

PROJECT: THE THOUGHT MOSAIC
For when you want to feel like a gardener of ideas

WHAT: Create a vibrant and thought-provoking mosaic made up of the different voices of students at your school.

Difficulty Rating: 5

1 = easy peasy
2 = a little tricky
3 = thinking cap on
4 = kind of complicated
5 = requires serious brain power

WHERE: A school hallway, on a wall in the cafeteria, at an after-school hotspot.

WHY: The students at your school may see the same group of kids day in and day out, but how well do they actually know each other? The Thought Mosaic is a cool, visual way to capture the unique perspective of your classmates while making a bold statement at the same time. Namely: We are all separate, complicated pieces that when put together, make a powerful, sometimes unexpected, whole.

WHAT YOU NEED

• Paper that will be cut into shapes (feel free to get creative and use different types and colors too!)

• A way to hang the responses and set your space apart, such as tape or ribbon

• Dark markers that will show up well on colored paper*

HOW TO DO IT

1. Come up with your questions: Write down a few questions you want other students to answer or creative prompts for things kids could write about. Some ideas: *What makes you feel happy? What makes you feel hopeful? What's one thing you wish adults understood about kids like you? What is your favorite aspect of YOU? What's your secret (or strange) talent?*

2. Pitch your idea: You'll need the school's okay to move forward, so formally propose your idea to a teacher you think

BECOME IMMORTAL (WELL, YOUR *PROJECT*, ANYWAY)

Your Thought Mosaic might not be able to stay up forever, but that doesn't mean it can't live on for all eternity! Find a way to capture it—scrapbook, photobook, video or slideshow, collage—to keep the goodness going long into the future. Think of it as a community time capsule.

---

* You'll also need the support of a teacher or school administrator when it comes time to choose locations and executing

might be interested in helping you out and ask them to be your official adviser for the project.

3. Come up with your plan: Is this a once and done kinda thing? Or an ongoing project with new themes covered each week? Can students participate on their own, or will you need volunteers to hand out paper and pens? (Don't forget to run your plan by your adviser.)

4. Gearing up: Gather your supplies, decide when and where to share your idea with the kids at school, and get everything ready for launch.

BONUS TIP:
When you create an art project like this in school, there's always the chance that some kids will post gross or inappropriate things. (I know, hard to believe, right?) My suggestion? Have rules for participation, spelling out exactly what is and isn't okay (e.g. swear words, crude pictures, or hate speech are a no go). The truth is, every garden is going to have some weeds . . . pull them out!!

5. Grow your garden of ideas: Whether your project happens at a certain time or it's ongoing, set up your writing station and get started!

6. Document it: As your garden of ideas grows, take pictures, shoot a video, write notes, or document it in some other way. You'll want to be able to look back on what you did after the project ends (and you might even be able to use it in a cool way).

TENDING TO THE GARDEN

Just as gardeners have to frequently check in with their plants to deal with changes in the weather, pesky critters, and weeds, when we're doing public art like the Thought Mosaic, we need to keep a close eye on things.

- **Observe:** While your project is running, notice what's working and what isn't, and listen to what other students are saying. Depending on what you see and hear, you may tweak the project or discover something else exciting to explore and adjust your direction.

- **Speak Up:** If some students are making a joke of what you're doing, don't be afraid to ask them to stop being a part of it. It may just not be their thing, and that's perfectly fine.

- **Keep Going:** If the project is unfolding the way you hoped, that's great! Keep on keepin' on! And if not, don't be afraid to switch it up and try a different approach.

- **Collect:** Ask students to submit the themes they'd like to see expressed on the wall and choose the one you're most interested in for the next round. And don't forget to think about the class as a whole when you're making your choice (meaning, don't play favorites and pick your BFF's idea!).

- **Check In:** Meet with your teacher/adviser when the project is over to talk about how you think everything went. Can the project expand? Is it time to stop? What's next, if anything?

PROJECT: APPRECIATION TOKENS

*For when you want to show others
that what they do matters*

WHAT: Create your own
Appreciation Tokens and hand
them out anytime you see someone
doing a kind act to show them you
appreciate who they are!

Difficulty Rating: 2

1 = easy peasy
2 = a little tricky
3 = thinking cap on
4 = kind of complicated
5 = requires serious
   brain power

WHERE: Anywhere at school,
including in student groups, on
sports teams, and in after-school clubs or extracurriculars.

WHY: People do good things for others every single day, but
it sometimes feels like the negative stuff gets all the attention.
This project lets you flip the script and shine a spotlight on the
awesome and generous things people around you are doing.
Who knows . . . you just might start a kindness epidemic!

TIPS TO MAKE YOUR TOKENS STAND OUT

Your tokens can look however you'd like, so unleash your
creative side! Here are some ideas to get you started:

• Ask a teacher to help you laminate the paper after you've
made your design. This will help them be more durable so
they can be shared over and over.

• Use different colors and materials to make each token pop.
(But watch out for glitter. It gets everywhere, amiright!?).

WHAT YOU NEED
• Material to make the tokens like paper, cardstock, cardboard (feel free to get creative and use different types, colors, and shapes)
• Pencils, pens, or markers

HOW TO DO IT
1. Craft your tokens: Here are some things to consider before you get grooving:
• What do I want the tokens to look like?
• How many should I make?
• What should they say?
• Should they all say the same thing (e.g., "you're awesome!") or should I personalize each one (e.g. "you stood up for someone who was being bullied" or "you helped someone when you didn't have to")?

2. Get giving: It's time to step back, observe your classmates, and show your appreciation when someone does something totally token-worthy. I betcha when you start looking, you'll see good things happening everywhere.

3. Use your head: After a day or week of handing out Appreciation Tokens, take a pause to think about what's working well and what could use some tweaking. Focus on the highlights and use those to keep you going. And as always, be flexible and make adjustments as you need to.

BONUS TIP:
We all get by with a little help from our friends, so why not ask a few to join in and help you out? After all, a few extra sets of eyes = more good deeds spotted!

WANT TO GO BIGGER?

Trust me—this is one of those projects teachers tend to like. Why? Because it encourages kindness and being an awesome human, and I know for sure that's one cause a teacher can fully get behind! So why not tap into this support to help your work evolve? For instance, your teacher might add his or her own incentives as a way of encouraging classmates to give and receive Appreciation Tokens.

MY FAVORITE WAY TO HAND OUT APPRECIATION TOKENS

There's something to be said for silent appreciation. In fact, when I do this project, I prefer to quietly give someone a token and simply walk away. How you hand them out is totally your call—do what feels right for you. But if you believe silence is golden, remember that you don't need to say anything at all to show someone you appreciate who they are. (Of course, if people are looking for an explanation, by all means, fill them in!)

PROJECT: LETTER TO_____

*For when you want to bring a group together
to share complicated feelings*

When we think about writing letters, we usually think about writing to one specific person. But letters are great ways to express yourself—and sometimes writing things out can help you better understand how you feel at a given moment—

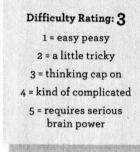

Difficulty Rating: 3

1 = easy peasy

2 = a little tricky

3 = thinking cap on

4 = kind of complicated

5 = requires serious
    brain power

so in tough times, why not join together as a community to write to a place, object, idea, or emotion?

WHAT: Join with others in your community to write a letter about a topic that concerns you all.

WHERE: During lunch, recess, or any other free period in school when you can wander freely and talk to other students, teachers, and staff members.

WHY: Sometimes it's hard to know if other people in your community have the same feelings you do. It can be hard even to name feelings unless someone else starts the conversation. It can be easier to express feelings in writing and when someone has already started the conversation.

WHAT YOU NEED:
- Pens, pencils, or markers
- Paper

For more real-world inspiration, check out the World Letter project by musician and performance artist Cocovan. Visit her website at www.theworldletter.com.

HOW TO DO IT

1. Think about what you want to write to. Is it a place that you've heard about in your class or in the news that is going through a difficult time? Is it an emotion that you know many of your classmates are experiencing—for instance, stage fright before a class play? Or is it an object that symbolizes something important to you?

2. Get your materials together and write "Dear [your subject here]" in big letters at the top of the paper.

3. Encourage other people to participate by writing your own feelings in the first sentence.

PRO TIPS: TO MAKE THE MOST OF THIS EXPERIENCE
- Make sure your contributors are okay with the possibility of the letter being put on public display when it is done.

- Ask a trusted adult to be your consultant on this one, and check in with them along the way. They can direct contributors to resources that can help with hard feelings.

4. **Figure out how you want to collect other people's contributions for the letter.** If you don't mind other students knowing that you started the project, you can take your paper from person to person and ask them to write something. If you would prefer to remain anonymous, ask a teacher if there is an area in the school where you can hang the paper and if they will help you to spread the word to students, teachers, and staff about the project.

5. **Decide what to do with your letter** when you are done. Should it hang in your school? Should it live on social media— on an Instagram or a Facebook page? Maybe you want to share it with a local publication. There are lots of places to go!

6. **Think about how the project went.** Do you want to do a new letter? How might you reach more people?

EXTRA IDEA ALERT: PROBLEM-SOLVING SQUAD

WAIT! Before you move on, there's one more thing to say about school. So here it is: I know that school life can sometimes involve tough stuff—bullying, feeling alone, social drama, feeling like you can't be you without sticking out like a sore thumb. The great news is, community art projects can address all of these issues. Don't get me wrong—you alone are a force to be reckoned with. But when you join forces with some big-hearted friends? You will be unstoppable. Tap into the power of numbers to make some serious change.

FIRST, UNCOVER THE PROBLEMS . . .
- **Look Around:** What types of challenges are other kids at school facing?
- **Get Curious:** What's behind the problems? How might they be solved?

NEXT, RALLY THE TROOPS . . .
- **Gather Your Crew:** Find your peeps who care about the same issues and are inspired to help you tackle the challenges.
- **Get Creative:** Get together and brainstorm ways to solve the problem(s). Share ideas, ask questions, set goals.

LAST, GET TO WORK . . .
- **Create Your Plan:** Work together to craft your problem-solving strategy, making sure everyone knows the next steps and is working toward the same thing.
- **Keep Going!** Meet regularly as a group to check in on progress, cheer each other on, and plan for more good deeds!

CHAPTER 6

PROJECTS IN THE COMMUNITY

I'll fess up. This is probably my favorite chapter in the whole book. Because, in my opinion, doing our art out in the community is where it's at. Sharing our unique thoughts, ideas, and POV with other people from every walk of life? Now that is really our chance to not only leave our artistic footprint in the world, but be agents of positive change.

Seriously. Think of yourself as a Secret Agent of Change. But instead of donning a mask or utility belt, your project is the costume. And get this—your disguise is so good, people won't even realize they're being challenged or inspired or motivated or changed by participating. It will just happen. And all because you created the opportunity. (Seriously. If that's not the coolest thing, I don't know what is.)

Here's why bringing your off-the-charts energy and drive into your community is so important:

A. Your voice matters. Some people think that no one listens to what kids have to say, but in my experience, the exact opposite is true. Your voice has the potential to be so much louder exactly because you're a kid. You doing your art in the world can throw people off-guard in an amazing way. And since they're not expecting it, people tend to sit up and take notice.

B. There are literally no limits to where you (and your art) can go. Seriously. The world may be immense, but as a society we've never been more connected than we are today. (I'll spare you the whole, "When I was your age, we didn't even have cell phones!" thing. But it's true! And I'm not even that old!) A tiny movement you start in your community—yes, even right there in the middle of Everytown, USA—has the potential to change someone's life halfway around the world. Don't believe me? Try it out and see for yourself.

C. You can have an effect right now. No sitting around twiddling your thumbs, thank you very much. Political, social, environmental—whatever you're passionate about, you can push the needle forward and literally be the change.

So what do you say? Are you ready to give one (or more)

of these projects a shot? Because I'll let you in on a secret: changing the world isn't hard. All it takes is doing things to make things happen. So, my friend, be a doer.

PROJECT: FAMILIAR FACES

For when you want to feel like a photographer and capture something special

---

WHAT: Become a community photographer by taking portrait-style pictures of people in your neighborhood, town, or city and then hosting a public photography show of your work.

> **Difficulty Rating: 5**
>
> 1 = easy peasy
> 2 = a little tricky
> 3 = thinking cap on
> 4 = kind of complicated
> 5 = requires serious brain power

WHERE: Any spot where you're inspired by the people you come across, such as a local coffee shop, a town square, the library, the mall, a retirement home, a community center, a bus stop.

WHY: There's so much more to other people than what we see at first glance, especially the strangers we pass by every day. By sharing your portraits, you'll help other people see and connect with one another on a more human level.

PRO TIP: If you don't know how to use a camera, join forces with someone who does. Not only can they help you with your project, but you might also learn some photography skills to boot!

PRO TIP: If you're displaying your pictures in a public place, write an artist's statement explaining your project and post it near the photos. Professional artists do this to help people understand why they created what they did.

WHAT YOU NEED
- camera (if you have access to a regular camera, awesome; if not, a camera on a phone can do the trick)
- tripod (optional)
- computer (optional)
- homemade sign explaining what you're doing

HOW TO DO IT
1. Set the spot: Where do you want to do this project? Think about these questions to figure it out:
- What's my favorite place?
- Where might people be open to being photographed?
- Where would I like to help people feel more connected and a part of something?

2. Decide on your end goal: Do you want to showcase your photos in a "gallery" exhibit? A slideshow you'll screen for people? Sharing on Instagram? (Or maybe even all of the above!)

3. Ask around: Talk to the important people you'll need to deal with, such as the owner of the camera or the manager of the place where you want to do your photo shoot. Gather as much info ahead of time as possible.

4. Prep for the shoot: Get organized for the big day by going through the following checklist:
- ☐ Choose date for the event
- ☐ Gather your supplies
- ☐ Give everyone involved a heads-up about what's happening and when
- ☐ Officially ask permission from the person in charge of your hoped-for location

5. Prep your gear: Make a sign explaining your project, charge your camera, and pack up your tripod and other gear so you're ready to go.

TIPS FOR MAKING YOUR PHOTO SHOOT ROCK:

• Lighting matters a lot in photography—scope out the scene ahead of time and figure out how you'll get the best light. Make sure to do it at the same time of day that you plan on taking photos, so you'll be able to see what the crowds are like then and what the natural light looks like.

• If your location is near a business, set up where you won't be in the way of customers.

• Remember that the best spot for your "photo booth" might actually be outside the location.

• Watch online videos from photography pros to pick up some quick tips and tricks.

• If you're using a camera you aren't used to, practice. Family and friends (and maybe even pets) make great test models.

6. **Lights, camera, action!** Set up your photo station at the location, hang up your sign, and start taking pictures!

7. **Put it all together:** After you're finished with the photo shoot, create your final project in the way you planned in step two. If you're sticking with social media, start sharing your Instagram account (or maybe even create a new one just for this project). If you're making a slideshow, put it together and add music or titles if that's your jam. And if you're going old-school gallery, print out your photos and set up your exhibit (a great spot is the place where you took them!).

TIPS FOR A SUCCESSFUL PHOTO SHOOT:

- The number one reason why someone might not participate in a project is because they weren't asked! If people aren't volunteering to get their picture taken, don't be shy. Tell them what you're doing and ask them to join in.

- See if the staff at your location will encourage customers to participate. For instance, if you're set up outside Starbucks, ask a barista if she'll say to customers, "While you're waiting for your coffee, you might want to get your picture taken!" (You'd be surprised at how willing people are to help.)

- To go deeper, gather info from your photo subjects by asking them a simple question or two, like "Where are you from?" or "What's your name?" Pairing the photos with these answers will make the exhibit feel more personal. What other questions could you ask?

BONUS TIP: If your project will cost you money (for instance, if you need to buy frames for pictures or get color printouts of your images), consider setting up a donation box with your photography studio. Just be specific about how you'll use the donations and thank people when they make a contribution!

PROJECT: CHAIN REACTION
For when you want to start a whole movement

WHAT: Talk to people in your community about a topic you are passionate about, and give them a visual reminder of the conversation. Soon you'll see people all around your community with the same visual cue.

Difficulty Rating: 4
1 = easy peasy
2 = a little tricky
3 = thinking cap on
4 = kind of complicated
5 = requires serious brain power

WHERE: A community center, a grocery store, a coffee shop, a mall—anywhere that you might see a lot of people.

WHY: When people are walking down the street, you never know what is on their mind. By giving people a way to outwardly identify that they care about a topic, you are opening avenues of conversation for your whole community.

WHAT YOU NEED
• thick ribbon
• marker

HOW TO DO IT
1. Choose a topic: Think about something that you are passionate about. It could be a big political topic that affects the world, or it might be a local topic that affects just your neighborhood. Learn everything you can about it to prepare for

your conversations—read articles, watch the news— maybe you can even interview someone who is involved to get their take on the subject!

2. Identify a location:

Think about where you want to be for this project. You want to pick a place that has people passing by regularly—

somewhere that is busy enough so you will have people to talk to, but not so crowded that you will be lost among all of the people.

3. Prepare your materials:

This project will be easiest to do if everything is in order ahead of time, so cut your ribbons into bracelet-size pieces. Make sure you make them bigger than you think you might need—some people have big wrists or will want to wear their bracelets loosely.

DON'T GET DISCOURAGED!

This is hard work! It can be hard to get folks to stop and talk—they might be busy, or they might not understand at first exactly what you're trying to do. But don't give up! Every interaction is one you can learn from. If people don't respond to your question, try starting a conversation a different way. Art is a process, so feel free to adjust.

4. Start a chain reaction!

a. Go to your location and ask people walking by to talk with you about your cause. Be polite and ask something like "Excuse me, do you have a moment to speak?" Tell them that you are doing a community art project and want to discuss your topic. Then ask if they have any opinions they would like to share.

b. Remember that the point of this is to hear other opinions, so let the people you are communicating with take the lead in the conversation. Listen closely and ask questions. You can share your opinions, too, but you want to hear from them first.

c. After a few minutes of conversation, thank the person for their time and ask if you can give them a token of your appreciation. If they say yes, then write a word or phrase that came up in your conversation on the ribbon and tie it around their wrist. Ask them to use that bracelet as a reminder of your conversation and to keep that conversation going with others.

PROJECT: LIVING CARTOONS
*For warming up and getting used to making art in public—
and for getting a little silly!*

WHAT: Draw pictures of characters and ask others to write what the characters are saying.

WHERE: Anywhere with a lot of foot traffic—outside a store or coffee shop, for example, or at the local library. Don't forget to ask permission before setting up!

Difficulty Rating: 2

1 = easy peasy
2 = a little tricky
3 = thinking cap on
4 = kind of complicated
5 = requires serious brain power

WHY: It can be scary to go into a new place to make art! Start out with this easy project to get used to talking to people.

WHAT YOU NEED
- paper
- pens, crayons, markers
- a table and a chair

HOW TO DO IT

1. Scope out a location: Find a spot with lots of good foot traffic. Ask for permission to set up your project and figure out the best time to do it.

2. Prepare materials ahead of time: At home, draw a few characters on different sheets of paper. How different can you make them look? Think about hair styles, accessories, and all the other fun features that make us individuals. Draw conversation bubbles above their heads, but don't fill in the dialogue yet. You'll make more drawings later, but these will help you starting out.

3. Set up your table: On the day of your project, set up your table with extra paper, pencils, markers, and crayons. Lay out your first drawings and write something in the dialogue bubble of one of the characters.

4. Start a conversation: Ask passersby to write their own comments in the word bubbles. How would one character react to the other? Can a whole conversation get started here?

5. Draw more: Get inspired by the people passing by and draw even more characters.

TAKE IT UP A NOTCH:

• Ask passersby to draw their own characters for other people to write comments on.

• Cut out quotations from an old magazine or newspaper and ask passersby to draw characters to match the quotations.

• Don't forget about pets—what might they say?

PROJECT: A TABLE AND TWO CHAIRS

For when you want to feel helpful or channel your inner actor

---

I promise this one isn't too hard, but it does require the P-word. You know . . . patience. This project is sort of like fishing—you might sit around for a long time without a bite, but half the fun is just being out there.

Difficulty Rating: 4

1 = easy peasy

2 = a little tricky

3 = thinking cap on

4 = kind of complicated

5 = requires serious brain power

WHAT: Set up your own "office" in your neighborhood, community park, or other central spot in your town and invite people who pass by to have a seat and talk with you about anything you like.

WHERE: Any spot where there's a steady flow of people—in front of your home, at a park, or outside a local café, coffee shop, or sports stadium.

WHY: Sometimes people want nothing more than to share something on their mind and be genuinely heard. It doesn't matter if you're twelve, twenty-two, fifty-two, or a hundred and two—you can bring something positive to the people around you by simply being there.

WHAT YOU NEED
- one table
- two chairs
- homemade sign explaining what you're doing
- trusted adult for support
- optional: any other "art" for your office

HOW TO DO IT
1. Brainstorm your gig: To get clear on how you want to move forward, answer the following questions:
- What do I want to get out of doing this?
- What do I want other people to get out of it?
- Should I dress up and make it a performance, or just show up as me?
- Where could I set up my office?
- What kind of things do I want to talk about with people? (ie.g. Do I want to give advice? Tell jokes? Answer any questions they have? Share random trivia?) Hint: There's no right or wrong . . . get creative!

2. Talk it out: Let your family and friends in on your plan (remember, some of them may not "get it," but that's okay), as well as anyone you'll need to get permission from, like the owner of the business where you want to set up shop.

3. Plan how you'll share: Decide how you'll spread the word about your experience. Write a blog post? Ask a friend to snap photos and share with a unique hashtag or Instagram account?

- Prep for your first day: Use the following checklist to make sure you have all your ducks in a row and are ready to go:
    - ☐ Set the date(s) you want to set up your office
    - ☐ Decide how long your office will be open
    - ☐ Confirm your plan with the necessary people
    - ☐ Get your office supplies ready
    - ☐ Figure out how you'll get your table and chairs to your location
- Get Out There! Set up your office at the location, hang up your sign, and have fun!

PERFORMANCE ART?

When I do Subway Therapy, I always wear my suit (and let me just say I'm not usually a suit kinda guy). I wear it because it helps me get into character for my project. Yes, I'm still me, but in my suit I feel a little different, and more professional. As you develop your project, remember that you don't have to be you, per se. If you're feeling adventurous, you can dress up or create a fun theme for your office . . . you can even use a fake name. When you do this, your project becomes more of a performance.

GROW YOUR WORK

A Table and Two Chairs is the kind of project you might do just once, or you might want to continue doing it, like me! If you're in it for the long haul, be willing to switch it up every now and then if your gut, or your participants, send you the signal it's time for something new.

P.S. This project is how it all started for me—just a table and two chairs. And check it out now . . . you're reading my book!

STUCK WITH A CHATTY CATHY? MY TIPS FOR (POLITELY) WRAPPING UP A CONVERSATION

Sometimes people get so caught up talking with you that they don't realize it's time to finish the conversation and give someone else a chance to talk. I know. I've been there. Here's what I do . . . It works (almost) every time!

> You: What was your name again?
>
> Them: Talkative Tom.
>
> You: Tom, it was nice talking with you today. Thanks for stopping by!
>
> Them: It was nice talking with you too!

Or

> You: It's been nice talking with you, but I'd like to see if I can talk with a few more people before I'm finished today. Maybe you can come by again next time I'm here?

IMPORTANT TIPS FOR STAYING SAFE IN STICKY SITUATIONS

- **Don't feel bad saying no.** If someone asks you for personal info about yourself or anything else you're not comfortable sharing, here's your go-to line: Thanks for asking, but I don't talk about certain things while I'm at this table.

- **Trust your gut.** If the conversation is getting weird or you're feeling pressured to say things you don't want to, here's your go-to line: I need to think for a bit, and I don't want to talk anymore.

- **Be ready to walk away.** When you're interacting with the public, you need to be ready to just walk away. If something bad or scary happens, here's your go-to action: If you're in front of a coffee shop or business, just walk inside. If you're in a park or outdoor space, have someone you know nearby and give them the signal you need help.

- **Take time to process.** After you're finished, take time for yourself to think about how it went before you do anything else:

- **Reflect** on what worked well and what didn't work so well.

- If you took notes, read them!

- If people took photos, look for them on social media.

- Think about how you want to move forward . . . then start planning!

CHAPTER 7

SPREADING THE WORD

Well, here we are . . . the last chapter! Phew! Time flies when you're having fun. Let's recap: You've explored your identity as an artist, you've learned that being an artist is really about being a scientist, a detective, and an explorer, and you've tackled community art projects that can make a bold statement and change the world. Simply put, you came, you created, you conquered. Well done!

But before you go, there are just a few last things we need to talk about. First, doing these kinds of projects and dealing with people you don't know comes with some big responsibilities and safety considerations. And second, I have some ideas I wanna share about how to get the word out so your art can have an even bigger effect. Read on to learn how to practice your "creative street smarts" when you're out there in the big, wide world, as well as discovering my best tips for helping your art and message spread.

CREATIVE STREET-SMART TIPS

TIP #1: SAFETY FIRST

If your art was going into a museum, the rules would be pretty simple: create art + give to museum = BOOM . . . done. But since participatory art happens in a public space, it's not so simple.

Reality check: Sometimes the world can be a complicated and tough place, so it's important to be smart and protect yourself while you're out there being a change-maker. Here are some tips:

- **Do Your Homework:** Have you ever gotten called on in class when you weren't listening? Doesn't feel great, right? You want to be prepared for your art project the same way you are for school. So gather as much intel ahead of time as possible about the place you're planning to do your project so you're ready for anything.

- **Follow the Law:** Respecting the rules about things like trespassing, soliciting, hours of operation, and vandalism will keep you out of trouble. 'Nuff said.

- **Get Permission:** Be aware of instances where you may need to lock in permission to do your thing and plan ahead to get it. When in doubt: ask.

- **Bring Along a Friend:** Fact: it's not safe to go solo in certain environments. Always bring along a partner if you're unsure about the vibe of a place or choose a very public spot where there will be plenty of people nearby.

- **Always Have a Plan:** Decide ahead of time what you'll do if something goes wrong—who you'll call and where you'll go.

- **Trust Your Gut:** Pay attention to that voice in your head that pipes up when something feels uncomfortable or dangerous. If you sense something isn't right, take care of yourself by walking away or getting help.

TIP #2: KEEP COOL IF YOUR WORK IS COPIED

When you put your art out into the world, it's really out there. Meaning, other people can see, share, enjoy, and be inspired by your idea. At the same time, that means they can copy your idea too. And here's the kicker . . . their project might even be more successful than yours. (I know, right?) It happens. The truth is, sometimes creative ideas bounce around—it's possible that another person had the same idea as you at the exact same time. You know, like the time you and your best friend wore the same outfit to school and everyone assumed it was intentional when in reality it was so not planned.

Whatever the case, trust me when I say being copied by someone else isn't the end of the world. When you think about it, it's kind of flattering that another person likes your idea enough to do the same thing themselves. If this does happen, you can do what I do and say to yourself, "Hey, I inspired that person, so what I'm doing must be pretty good!"

Bottom line: No one else can create the art you would create. Focus on slaying with your own idea.

TIP #3: FIND A VIRTUAL MENTOR

Forging a new path with your art is exciting, but there's always something to be learned from the movers and shakers who are already out there changing the world through their work. Why not tap into all that hard-won wisdom by reaching out to some of your biggest inspirations? It's really as simple as: a) thinking about who you want to connect with, b) figuring out what you'd like to learn from them, and c) making your art. You never know what kind of brilliance you might get back.

Intimidated? Unsure? Convinced you'll never get a reply? I totally understand. But I challenge you to go for it anyway.

QUICK TIPS FOR REACHING OUT TO PEOPLE YOU DON'T KNOW (BUT WANT TO)

- **Be respectful:** Email, tweet, or message with humility, kindness, and respect. Think simple requests, not demands. In my experience, a little courtesy goes a long way.

- **Make it easy for people to say yes:** People are more likely to respond to requests they can act on quickly and easily (e.g. What's one piece of advice you can share? Or Would you be willing to tweet out my project to your followers?). The bigger and more complicated the ask, the less likely you'll hear back.

- **Think persistence, not pestering:** Following up in a week if you haven't gotten a response shows you're committed. Emailing daily (or hourly)? Not so much. If after a few tries all you're getting is crickets, it's probably time to move on.

- **Don't take it personally:** Not hearing back can be a bummer, but sometimes people get too busy to respond to every message. So approach your quest with cautious optimism, and don't take it personally if you don't hear back. (This is almost always a case of "it's not you, it's them!")

- **Reach out to more than one person:** It's simple math really—the more people you reach out to, the higher the chances someone will respond. So cast a wide net!

STEAL THIS EMAIL

Think of this as a fill-in-the-blank for reaching out cold to someone you admire:

Hi, [insert first name]!

My name is [insert your name], and I'm an [insert grade]-grade student from [insert hometown]. I am a big fan of your [insert specific writing, poetry, art, or music project here] and really admire the way you [highlight one or two specific things you love about the person]. Your [insert medium] has been very inspiring to me. I'm writing to ask if you would consider [insert your clear and easy-to-answer request]. I know you are very busy—thank you for considering this request! I look forward to hearing from you.

Best regards,

[insert your name]

Not sure how to get in touch? Start by checking out the creator's website (if they have one) and find their contact form or email address. If you come up empty, try their social media profiles.

ARE YOU READY TO GO VIRAL?

So you wanna go big or go home? Do you have dreams of your video going viral or your community art project being featured on the local news? Many artists create their work hoping for this kind of attention, and that's totally cool! Sometimes, like what happened with Subway Therapy, it happens when you least expect it. Of course, like most everything in life, there are no guarantees. It's true. There's just no way to know whether or not your idea will catch on.

Though you may not be able to predict the future, there are ways to increase the chances that your project will take off, as well as get yourself prepared for whatever comes next. Read on and I'll show you how.

MAKING YOUR OWN LUCK

So you might be wondering, if there's no way to make something take off, does that mean a project's success is really just a case of right time, right place (aka luck)? I won't lie . . . sometimes there's a little bit of luck at play. But rather than sit around waiting for luck to strike, you can make your own. How? You create the right place. And you commit to being there at the right time.

I'm not saying you have to spend every moment of every day working on your art (your parents and teachers might have a few things to say about that . . .). What I mean is that you've got to own it. Be consistent. Be all in. Go for it, big time. The people out there totally crushing it in their fields? People like Justin Timberlake, Serena Williams, and Elon Musk? That's what they do. When you own it, other people will notice your passion and persistence, and that's when the momentum can really start picking up. (P.S. That same thing is true for anything you want to do in life. Step up to the plate with confidence and swing, baby, swing!)

GOING SOCIAL WITH YOUR ART

Social media is good for so much more than chatting with friends and watching videos of adorable puppies. In fact, it can be one of the most useful tools out there for artists like us looking to amplify our work, not to mention connect with other like-minded people. But of course, not all social media is created equal. Here's a look at the most useful social media tools for creatives:

INSTAGRAM
A photo-sharing app that's a natural fit for highly visual creative projects.

- **Pros:** Great for pictures and video; powerful way to share your personal brand
- **Cons:** Can only post from phone; it can be hard to get noticed and find followers
- **Pro Tip:** Post consistently and use popular #hashtags to get more eyes on your feed

DEALING WITH DOUBTERS

Confession: Some people think my art is strange or stupid. But I'm okay with that (really, I am), because I know my art isn't everybody's cup of tea. I know that's part of the deal with putting your art (and heart) out into the world—not everybody's gonna get it. The same thing might happen to you. But believe me when I say that if it does, it's totally normal. Sure, it can be hard not to take it personally when someone you respect doesn't get what you're doing. Just remember that people are going to feel how they're gonna feel, and their reaction actually has nothing to do with you.

FACEBOOK

A social media giant perfect for organizing and bringing people together.

- **Pros:** Great for organizing events; Facebook live videos are perfect for sharing in real-time; easy to build community
- **Cons:** Your audience might be made up of more grandparents than young people
- **Pro Tip:** Create a Facebook page for your project where you can post updates, share photos, get feedback, and directly connect with people interested in what you're up to

YOUTUBE

An online video-sharing platform ideal for performers, filmmakers, or anyone else with a point of view to share.

- **Pros:** Perfect for sharing videos of all kinds, from music performances and flash mobs to documentaries and interviews; great search engine makes it easy for people to find your

channel; YouTube stores your big video files for free
- **Cons:** Sometimes people leave rude and hurtful comments
- **Pro Tip:** Customize your YouTube channel with colors and images from your art and brand

TWITTER

The ultimate social media platform for sharing news and content in short 280-character sound bites.
- **Pros:** It's possible to connect with anyone via Twitter (as long as they have an account and are active on it)
- **Cons:** The lifespan of a tweet is only eighteen minutes, so you need to post consistently and frequently to be sure you're seen
- **Pro Tip:** Regularly retweet, like, and reply to tweets from the people you want to connect with to build up a relationship before going in for the ask

SO YOU'RE GETTING NOTICED . . . NOW WHAT?

All right, friend, here it is. You've worked your butt off putting your art out into the world, and now it's starting to gain attention. If you're like most people, you'll likely have one of the following reactions:

A. Jump right on it and ride the wave of popularity.

B. Feel both excited and nervous at the same time.

C. Be paralyzed with doubt and fear and hope the attention fades away.

PERMISSION TO ENTER

Have you ever seen a group of kids playing a game and a new kid comes along who clearly wants to join in but doesn't know how? The kid on the outside usually waits for someone to give them a signal—a look, a smile, an acknowledgment, a "hey you!"—before joining the game. The same thing happens with community art. Sometimes people will need your permission to step into the world you've created. So how can you help people get past the awkward should-I-or-shouldn't-I stage?

Don't worry—you don't need hand out permission slips. Giving others permission can be as easy as being approachable and nice. A genuine smile can go further than you could imagine. Other ideas for encouraging people to opt in are injecting a pinch of silliness, playing awesome music that gets people jamming, and having an icebreaker (a joke, a fun fact, an interesting question) at the ready.

All of these responses are normal, but one of them won't get you where you want to go. (I'm sure you can guess which one? Um, yes, people . . . I'm talking about C). The other two, A and B, are what you want to work toward, even if it feels a little scary.

When Subway Therapy took off, it got really big, really fast. Real talk: It was a little overwhelming. Even though I knew in my gut it was exactly what I should put all my energy into, keeping up with everything was hard and exhausting. But I'm so glad I stuck with it and didn't waste the opportunity. (In part because if I had, you wouldn't have gotten to read this book!)

Bottom line: When a cool opportunity pops up and that door standing in front of you is wide open, you've got to walk through it! It might be scary because you don't know what's on the other side or how things will work out. But when you follow your heart and your gut, that's when the real magic happens!

ALERT! LAST WORDS OF WISDOM! DO NOT SKIP! THIS IS GOOD STUFF!

Ladies and Gentlemen, here we are almost at the end of the book. I bet there's one thing you're still dying to know: Now that I'm ready, how do I get noticed? This is definitely one of the hardest things about becoming an artist in the world, but even though what I'm about to tell you isn't going to work like magic fairy dust, it will be pretty close. Ready? Cue the shining light and angelic voices! The ticket is to find your own thing.

If you remember only one message from this whole book, let it be this: your confidence, authenticity, and commitment will set you apart. Remember that no one can replicate the one and only you. And when you fully share your creative vision with the rest of us, the world will be better for it. One hundred percent.

You've got this. Now go on, get out there, and change the world through your art.